Reading Comprehension

Written by Dona Herweck Rice

Teacher Created Materials, Inc.
P.O. Box 1040
Huntington Beach, CA 92647
©1997 Teacher Created Materials, Inc.
Made in U.S.A.

ISBN 1-57690-249-8

Illustrator:
Barb Lorseyedi

Cover Artist:
Chris Macabitas

Editor:
Karen Goldfluss, M.S. Ed.

Imaging:
Ralph Olmedo, Jr.

Note to Parents and Teachers:

The books in this series were designed to help parents and teachers reinforce basic skills for their children and students. *Reading Comprehension* reviews basic reading skills for the second grade level. The exercises in this book can be done sequentially or can be taken out of order, as needed. In order to complete all exercises, children will need a pencil, crayons, scissors, and glue.

Here are some useful ideas for making the most of the books in this series.

- Remove the answer key and keep it for your own use.

- Help beginning readers with the instructions.

- Review the work the child has done. Whenever possible, work with the child.

- Allow the child to use whatever writing instruments he or she prefers. For example, colored pencils can add variety and pleasure to drill work.

- Pay attention to the areas in which the child has the most difficulty. Provide extra guidance and exercises in those areas.

Name _____

Complete each sentence with a word from the word box.

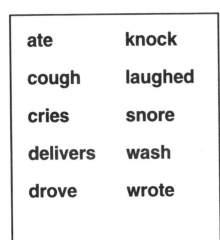

ate	knock
cough	laughed
cries	snore
delivers	wash
drove	wrote

1. Our mail carrier_____our mail early each morning.

2. I forgot to_____the dishes after dinner.

3. My cold made me _____and sneeze all night.

4. Did you see how fast he_____his race car?

5. I have never heard anyone _____as loudly as that!

6. The family_____pizza for dinner.

7. My neighbor_____a play for all of us to perform.

8. The doorbell is broken, so please_____.

9. The children_____at the circus clowns.

10. The puppy_____if we leave it alone.

Name _____

Draw lines to match the sentence from the first column that comes before the sentence in the second column.

The rabbit was too smart for the fox.	Now he can see much better.
We looked everywhere for our brother.	It hid in a hollow log and ran away when the fox passed by.
I like to play all kinds of games.	Stars twinkled all around.
The twins look exactly alike.	My favorite is hide-and-seek.
Emily saw a rainbow cross the entire sky.	We finally found him in the toy section of the department store.
The sky glowed in the moonlight.	Even their mother has a difficult time telling them apart.
The tiger crept through the tall grass and crouched in place.	Then it swiftly leapt at a nearby zebra.
Mr. Carter bought a new pair of glasses.	She thought she had never seen anything look so beautiful.

Name _____

Choose the meaning of the word as it is used in each sentence. Write the letter of the meaning used on the blank before the sentence.

play

   A. *take part in a game*
   B. *a story that is performed*
   C. *to make music with*

_____ 1. The actor prepared for opening night of the play.

_____ 2. Do you want to play hopscotch with me?

_____ 3. I can play the violin.

_____ 4. Who will play the piano during our concert?

_____ 5. I like to play imagination games.

run

   A. *move swiftly on foot*
   B. *operate*
   C. *stretch from place to place*

_____ 6. The repairman is going to run the line from the street to our house.

_____ 7. The athletes can run faster than anyone I have seen.

_____ 8. Can you run a sewing machine?

_____ 9. Did you see the dog run after the cat?

_____ 10. The woman in the booth is going to run the projector at the theater.

Name _____

Choose the meaning of the word as it is used in each sentence. Write the letter of the meaning used on the blank before the sentence.

call
A. *to say loudly*
B. *give a name to*
C. *short visit*

_____ 1. Did you call me?

_____ 2. You can call me Billy.

_____ 3. The teacher will call for the class to come inside.

_____ 4. My parents went to call on our neighbor.

_____ 5. We call our puppy Lucky.

well
A. *in good health*
B. *done in a good way*
C. *hole in the earth that fills with water*

_____ 6. My great-grandmother used to draw water from the family well.

_____ 7. I hope you are feeling well.

_____ 8. Jane, you have painted the room very well.

_____ 9. I stayed home from school because I was not well.

_____ 10. The family had to travel to the river because the well was dry.

Name _____

Number the pictures in order. Color the pictures.

Name _____

Color the pictures. Cut them out. Glue them in order.

1	2
3	**4**

8

Name _____

Read the sentences. Cut them out. Glue them in order.

They found a shady spot under a tree and ate lunch quickly.

At lunch time, Carl and Justin were both hungry.

The two children walked through the gate of the zoo early.

They spent the first two hours looking at the animals.

After lunch, it was time to go home.

Carl and Justin bought two tickets to the zoo.

Name _____

Write a sentence under each picture that tells the main idea of what is happening. Color the pictures.

Name _____

Read the paragraph below. Color the doctor's bag that has the main idea.

Eric and Maria want to work in a hospital when they grow

up. They read books about doctors, nurses, and the way

the body works. Every time they see a doctor or nurse,

they ask many questions about their jobs and what they

need to do in order to work in a hospital one day. They

never get tired of asking, and fortunately their doctors are

very patient! With so much research and interest, Eric and

Maria are sure to make wonderful hospital employees

one day.

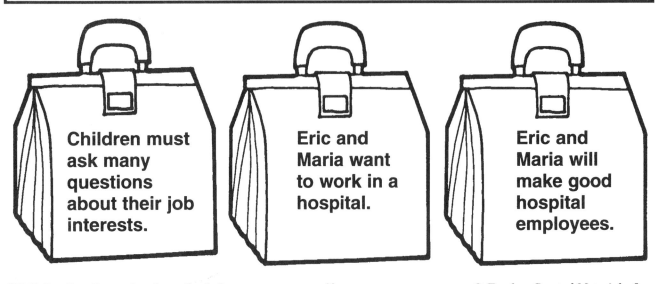

Children must ask many questions about their job interests.

Eric and Maria want to work in a hospital.

Eric and Maria will make good hospital employees.

Name _____

Read the paragraph below. Color the girl who has the main idea.

Amy did not do her arithmetic homework. She was going

to do it right after school, but a friend came over and they

watched television. When Amy's friend left, she asked her

mother if she could bake a pie for that night's dessert. She

made an apple pie. After dinner, Amy went to her room to

do her homework, but she discovered that she had left her

arithmetic book at school. She was sleepy, so she turned

out the light and went to bed early.

Amy forgot her arithmetic book at school.

Amy was too sleepy to do her arithmetic homework.

Amy did not do her arithmetic homework.

Name _____

Draw a picture that shows the main idea of each paragraph.

Kendra loves to read. She would keep her nose in a book at every minute if she could. It is no wonder that she got her first library card when she was only three years old. Reading is her favorite thing to do!

The kitten crept up to the ball of yarn like a tiger stalking its prey. First one paw and then the other, it kept its nose low to the ground and its eye on the ball. Every muscle was ready to jump.

Name _____

Sometimes, you can tell many things about a book by its cover. Look at the pictures on the covers below. Give each book a title that makes sense.

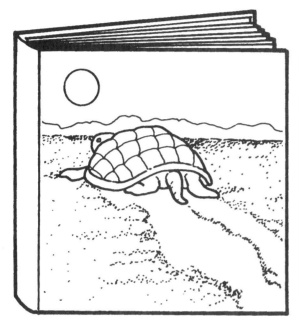

Title: _____

Title: _____
_____

Title: _____

Title: _____
_____

Name _____

Read the book titles. On each cover, draw a picture that makes sense.

Under the Sea

The Silly Rabbit

Name _____

Match each book title to its main idea.

No Television	A girl finds a dinosaur bone in her backyard.
George the Giraffe	An old key opens a secret door.
Follow the Star	A boy sets up an imaginary school for the neighborhood children.
The Mystery of the Broken Key	A lost girl finds her way by following the stars.
Saddles and Spurs	When the family television breaks, they all spend time together instead.
Fossils in the Neighborhood	Three children form a club to learn more about riding horses.
Sam's Summer Vacation	A make-believe giraffe has fun with his animal friends.
My Horse, Flash	A girl finally gets her wish, a horse.
Calvin Plays Teacher	A boy makes new friends at his summer camp.

Name _____

Read the story. Then answer the questions.

Pow! Stacie stared in disbelief as the ball sailed over the pitcher, second base, and finally past the outfield fence. It was a homerun, the first one she had ever hit! Dropping the bat at home plate, Stacie ran the bases one by one. Then she was home again, and the whole team rushed out to meet her.

1. What game is Stacie playing?

_____

2. How often does Stacie hit homeruns?

_____

3. What does the team do when Stacie comes home?

_____

Draw a picture from the story.

Name _____

Read the story. Then answer the questions.

Kenny woke up on Saturday morning and looked out the window. "It's raining!" he moaned and pulled the covers over his head. Just then, he felt a pounce on his feet and then on his stomach. He peeked out, and there was Buttons, purring and peeking back.

"Maybe it won't be such a bad morning, after all," Kenny thought, and petting Buttons, he jumped out of bed.

---

1. What kind of animal is Buttons?

   _____

2. How does Kenny feel about the rain?

   _____

3. What happens to cheer up Kenny?

   _____

Draw a picture from the story.

Name _____

Read the story. Then follow the directions below.

Marcus heard the music. "Listen!" he cried. "I hear it!" Marcus and his mother looked down the long street to their left. Only a moment later, they could see the band marching toward them. The bright red and blue uniforms sparkled almost as much as the shiny silver and gold instruments the musicians were playing.

As the band marched closer, Marcus looked at the instruments. He smiled when he saw the flutes. "Shawn should be coming by soon," he told his mother. After the flutes passed by, Marcus shouted, "There she is, Mom! There's Shawn!" He waved happily to his big sister.

When the parade was over, Marcus and his mother waited for Shawn to meet them. "You were great," he told Shawn.

"Thanks," Shawn answered. "I'm tired though. Let's go home!"

1. Circle the letter that happened first.

    A. Marcus saw the band.

    B. Marcus heard music.

    C. Shawn went home.

2. Circle the letter that happened after Marcus saw the flutes.

    A. He knew the trumpets would be next.

    B. He hugged his mother.

    C. He told his mother that he could see Shawn.

Name _____

Read the story. Then follow the directions below.

Kelly was cleaning her room. She found two small buttons, one large button, and an old sock that had a hole in it. She decided to use the things she had found to make a puppet. After she finished cleaning her room, she carried the sock and buttons to her mother. "May I make a puppet with these?" she asked.

Her mother smiled and said, "Yes, and you can also use the yarn in the sewing basket."

Kelly got the yarn and some glue. She carefully glued the buttons onto the sock so that they looked like two eyes and a nose. After that, she added yarn for hair. Finally, she put the puppet on her hand. What a great toy! Kelly rushed to show her mother her new puppet.

1. Circle what Kelly did after she finished cleaning her room.

    A. Kelly put the puppet on her hand.

    B. Kelly found some buttons.

    C. Kelly took the buttons and sock to show her mother.

2. Circle what Kelly did last.

    A. Kelly showed the puppet to her mother.

    B. Kelly put the sock puppet on her hand.

    C. Kelly glued yarn on her puppet to make it look like hair.

Name _____

Read the poem. Then answer the questions.

Sing a song of sixpence, a pocket full of rye;

Four and twenty blackbirds baked in a pie.

When the pie was opened, the birds began to sing;

Now, was not that a dainty dish to
    set before the king?

The king was in his counting house,
    counting out his money;

The queen was in the parlor, eating
    bread and honey.

The maid was in the garden,
    hanging out the clothes

When down came a blackbird and
    pecked off her nose.

1. How many blackbirds are in the pie? _____

_____

2. What do the birds do when the pie is opened? _____

_____

3. What is the king doing? _____

_____

4. Where is the queen?_____

_____

5. What happens to the maid? _____

_____

Name _____

Read the poem. Then answer the questions.

There was a crooked man,

And he walked a crooked mile.

He found a crooked sixpence

Against a crooked stile.

He bought a crooked cat,

Which caught a crooked mouse.

And they all lived together

In a little crooked house.

1. Who walked a mile? _____

_____

2. What did he find? _____

_____

3. What did he buy? _____

_____

4. What did the cat do?_____

_____

5. What does everything in the poem have in common? _____

_____

Name _____

Read the poem. Then answer the questions.

Old King Cole
Was a merry old soul,
And a merry old soul was he.
He called for his pipe,
And he called for his bowl,
And he called for his fiddlers three.
Every fiddler, he had a fiddle,
And a very fine fiddle had he.
Oh, there is none so rare
As can compare
With King Cole and his fiddlers three.

1. What sort of person is old King Cole? _____

_____

2. What is the second thing King Cole calls for? _____

_____

3. How many fiddlers are there?_____

_____

4. What kind of fiddles do the fiddlers have? _____

_____

5. List two pairs of rhyming words from the poem._____

_____

Name _____

Read the story. Then write the things that the polar bear does each day in order on the lines below.

The zookeeper at the Riverside Zoo was telling the children about the polar bear. "What does the polar bear do each day?" asked Paul.

"The polar bear swims, eats, plays, and sleeps," answered the zookeeper.

Paul thanked the zookeeper for his answer, but he was still curious. "When does the polar bear wake up?" How many times does he eat each day? Does he take naps? Does he stay awake all night?" Paul's questions went on and on.

"Oh, I see. You want details about how the bear lives his day, right?" said the zookeeper. "Well, let me see. He gets up at dawn because the light and the heat wake him. He usually goes for a swim right away. He gets out of the water when we feed him, which is at about ten o'clock. He takes a nap after he eats. After his nap, he usually swims again. Then he plays until about six o'clock, when we feed him again. He swims and plays until bedtime, which is as soon as it gets dark. Now do you understand about a polar bear's day in the zoo?"

"Yes, thank you," answered Paul. Then he turned to watch the polar bear with interest.

List the things the polar bear does each day. The first has been done for you.

1. He gets up at dawn.

2. _____

3. _____

4. _____

5. _____

6. _____

7. _____

8. _____

9. _____

Name _____

The first sentence of a paragraph often tells the main idea of the paragraph. The rest of the paragraph supports the main idea.

Read the paragraph below and then answer the questions.

You can learn to make friends. First, be friendly. Smile at other people and say, "Hello." Share your things. Be kind. Do not wait for others to talk to you. Go to them first, even if they do not seem interested at first. They may simply be shy. Take a chance! You are sure to make many friends.

1. What is the main idea of the paragraph?

   _____

   _____

2. How many ways does the paragraph suggest that you can make friends?

   _____

3. List three ways from the paragraph that you can make friends.

   _____

   _____

   _____

Name _____

Read the story. Then answer the questions.

Amy and Melanie wanted to earn some money to go to the movies. They tried washing dogs, but it was too messy. They tried babysitting, but it took too much time. So they decided to have a lemonade stand in front of their apartment building.

On a hot, dry, Saturday morning in June, the girls mixed the cold drinks in a plastic pitcher. They sold the lemonade drinks for one quarter each. Ten children and two adults bought the cold lemonade. Amy and Melanie each needed one dollar to get into the movies. Hooray! They were on their way!

1. Who is this story about?

_____

2. What two ways do they try to make money without any success?

_____

3. When do they open their lemonade stand?

_____

4. How much is a glass of lemonade?

_____

5. Do they get to go to the movies?

_____

Name _____

In order to find the main idea of a paragraph, you can ask yourself three questions:

Read the paragraph. Then answer the questions.

Lola loved to watch parrots. She liked to look at their bright green wings as they flew gracefully through the bird sanctuary, and she laughed when they called to each other in their loud, squeaky voices. Lola thought that parrots were the most wonderful animals ever created.

1. Who is this paragraph about?

   _____

2. What does she love to do?

   _____

3. Why does she love to do this?

   _____

Name _____

Read the paragraph. Write a who, what, and why question from the paragraph. Then answer the questions.

Jeffrey was afraid! His parents were not by the carousel. They were gone! Jeffrey had been with his parents, watching the funny characters as they walked by him. Now, when he looked up, his mother and father were nowhere to be seen. Jeffrey thought he was all alone at the amusement park.

Questions:

1. Who . . . _____

   _____

2. What . . . _____

   _____

3. Why . . . _____

   _____

Answers:

1. _____

   _____

2. _____

   _____

3. _____

   _____

Name _____

Read the paragraph. Write a who, what, and why question from the paragraph. Then answer the questions.

Jeffrey thought about what he should do. Then he remembered something that his parents had told him. "If you can't find us, you should tell someone who works at the amusement park. You will know that the person works here because he or she will be wearing a name tag." Jeffrey began searching for an adult with a name tag, and he had excellent luck. One was walking his way.

Questions:

1. Who . . . _____

   _____

2. What . . . _____

   _____

3. Why . . . _____

   _____

Answers:

1. _____

   _____

2. _____

   _____

3. _____

   _____

Answer Key

Page 2
1. delivers
2. wash
3. cough
4. drove
5. snore
6. ate
7. wrote
8. knock
9. laughed
10. cries

Page 3
The rabbit was too smart for the fox. It hid in a hollow log and ran away when the fox passed by.

We looked everywhere for our brother. We finally found him in the toy section of the department store.

I like to play all kinds of games. My favorite is hide-and-seek.

The twins look exactly alike. Even their mother has a difficult time telling them apart.

Emily saw a rainbow cross the entire sky. She thought she had never seen anything look so beautiful.

The sky glowed in the moonlight. Stars twinkled all around.

The tiger crept through the tall grass and crouched in place. Then it swiftly leapt at a nearby zebra.

Mr. Carter bought a new pair of glasses. Now he can see much better.

Page 4
1. B
2. A
3. C
4. C
5. A
6. C
7. A
8. B
9. A
10. B

Page 5
1. A
2. B
3. A
4. C
5. B
6. C
7. A
8. B
9. A
10. C

Page 6

Page 7
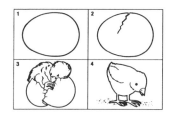

Page 9
Carl and Justin bought two tickets to the zoo.

The two children walked through the gate of the zoo early.

They spent the first two hours looking at the animals.

At lunch time, Carl and Justin were both hungry.

They found a shady spot under a tree and ate lunch quickly.

After lunch, it was time to go home.

Page 11
Sentences will vary. However, each sentence should logically reflect the picture.

Page 12
Eric and Maria want to work in a hospital.

Page 13
Amy did not do her arithmetic homework.

Page 14
The first picture should show a girl reading a book. The second should show a kitten ready to pounce on a ball of yarn.

Page 15
Titles will vary, but all should correspond directly with the pictures.

Page 16
Pictures will vary, but both should correspond directly with the titles.

Page 17
No Television = When the family television breaks, they all spend time together instead.

George the Giraffe = A make-believe giraffe has fun with his animal friends.

Follow the Star = A lost girl finds her way by following the stars.

The Mystery of the Broken Key = An old key opens a secret door.

Saddles and Spurs = Three children form a club to learn more about riding horses.

Fossils in the Neighborhood = A girl finds a dinosaur bone in her backyard.

Sam's Summer Vacation = A boy makes new friends at his summer camp.

My Horse, Flash = A girl finally gets her wish, a horse.

Calvin Plays Teacher = A boy sets up an imaginary school for the neighborhood children.

Answer Key (cont.)

Page 18
1. Stacie is playing baseball.
2. This is Stacie's first homerun. She does not hit them often.
3. The team rushes to meet Stacie at the plate.

The picture should accurately reflect an element of the story.

Page 19
1. Buttons is a cat.
2. Kenny does not like the rain. He is disappointed.
3. Buttons wants to play with Kenny and that cheers him up.

The picture should accurately reflect an element of the story.

Page 20
1. B
2. C

Page 21
1. C
2. A

Page 22
1. There are four and twenty (24) blackbirds.
2. The birds begin to sing.
3. The king is counting his money.
4. The queen is in the parlor.
5. A blackbird pecks off the maid's nose.

Page 23
1. The crooked man walked a mile.
2. He found a crooked sixpence.
3. He bought a crooked cat.
4. It caught a crooked mouse.
5. Some answers may vary, but the best answer is that they are all crooked.

Page 24
1. King Cole is a merry old soul.
2. King Cole calls for his bowl.
3. There are three fiddlers.
4. The fiddlers have very fine fiddles.
5. List any two of the following pairs: Cole/soul; he/three; Cole/bowl; soul/bowl; rare/compare.

Page 25
1. He gets up at dawn.
2. He goes for a swim.
3. At ten o'clock, he gets out of the water to eat.
4. He takes a nap.
5. He swims.
6. He plays.
7. At six o'clock, he eats again.
8. He swims and plays.
9. When it becomes dark, he goes to bed for the night.

Page 26
1. You can learn to make friends.
2. The paragraph suggests five ways to make friends.
3. Choose three from the following: smile; say, "Hello"; share; be kind; do not wait for others ; go to them first.

Page 27
1. The story is about Amy and Melanie.
2. They try washing dogs and babysitting.
3. They open their stand on a Saturday morning in June.
4. A glass of lemonade costs one quarter.
5. Yes, they can go to the movies.

Page 28
1. This paragraph is about Lola.
2. Lola loves to watch parrots.
3. She loves to do this because she thinks that parrots are the most wonderful animals ever created.

Page 29
The questions and answers will vary.

Page 30
The questions and answers will vary.